Inspiration

summersdale

INSPIRATION

Summersdale Publishers Ltd
46 West Street
Chichester
West Sussex
PO19 1RP
UK

www.summersdale.com

Printed and bound in China

ISBN: 978-1-84953-030-9

Substantial discounts on bulk quantities of Summersdale books are available to corporations, professional associations and other organisations. For details contact Summersdale Publishers by telephone: +44 (0) 1243771107, fax: +44 (0) 1243 786300 or email: nicky@summersdale.com.

Inspiration

thoughts & quotations
for every day

Know yourself and you will win all battles.

Sun Tzu

The greater the obstacle, the more glory in overcoming it.

Molière

Far away there in the sunshine are my highest aspirations. I may not reach them, but I can look up and see their beauty, believe in them, and try to follow where they lead.

Louisa May Alcott

If we wait for the moment when everything, absolutely everything is ready, we shall never begin.

Ivan Turgenev

First say to yourself what you would be;
and then do what you have to do.

Epictetus

Man's greatness lies in his power of thought.

Blaise Pascal

Fall seven times, stand up eight.

Japanese proverb

Some run swiftly; some creep painfully; all who keep on will reach the goal.

Piyadassi Thera

How wonderful it is that nobody need wait a single moment before starting to improve the world.

Anne Frank

Few things are impossible to diligence and skill. Great works are performed not by strength, but perseverance.

Samuel Johnson

*A journey of a thousand miles begins
with a single step.*

Lao Tzu

There is no chance, no destiny, no fate,
that can hinder or control the firm resolve
of a determined soul.

Ella Wheeler Wilcox

A man may fulfil the object of his existence by asking a question he cannot answer, and attempting a task he cannot achieve.

Oliver Wendell Holmes

Aim for the moon. If you miss, you may hit a star.

W. Clement Stone

The future belongs to those who believe in the beauty of their dreams.

Eleanor Roosevelt

Start by doing what's necessary; then do what's possible; and suddenly you are doing the impossible.

St Francis of Assisi

Life shrinks or expands in proportion to one's courage.

Anaïs Nin

A certain amount of opposition is a great help to a man. Kites rise against and not with the wind.

John Neal

A diamond with a flaw is worth more than a pebble without imperfections.

Chinese proverb

*Attempt the impossible
in order to improve
your work.*

Bette Davis

It is right to be contented with what we have, but never with what we are.

James Mackintosh

Better than a hundred years of idleness
Is one day spent in determination.

The Dhammapada

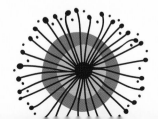

Never underestimate the power of passion.

Eve Sawyer

Satisfaction lies in the effort, not in the attainment. Full effort is full victory.

Mahatma Gandhi

*Life is a progress, and
not a station.*

Ralph Waldo Emerson

Fear is only as deep as the mind allows.

Japanese proverb

Whatever you do, do it with all your might.

Marcus Tullius Cicero

There is no impossibility to him who stands prepared to conquer every hazard.

Sarah J. Hale

Only those who have the patience to do simple things perfectly will acquire the skill to do difficult things easily.

Johann Friedrich von Schiller

The time is always right to do what is right.

Martin Luther King Jr

The people who get on in this world are the people who get up and look for the circumstances they want, and, if they can't find them, make them.

George Bernard Shaw

Regret for wasted time is more wasted time.

Mason Cooley

Dwell in possibility.

Emily Dickinson

*Talents are best nurtured in solitude,
but character is best formed in the stormy
billows of the world.*

Johann Wolfgang von Goethe

Nothing can stop the man with the right mental attitude from achieving his goal.

Thomas Jefferson

*To climb steep hills requires a slow
pace at first.*

William Shakespeare

The way to gain a good reputation is to endeavour to be what you desire to appear.

Socrates

All great achievements require time.

Maya Angelou

The only journey is the one within.

Rainer Maria Rilke

Collect as precious pearls the words of the wise and virtuous.

Abd al-Qādir

If you have an hour, will you not improve that hour, instead of idling it away?

Lord Chesterfield

If we all did the things we are capable of doing, we would literally astound ourselves.

Thomas A. Edison

Exert your talents, and distinguish yourself, and don't think of retiring from the world, until the world will be sorry that you retire.

Samuel Johnson

You must first be who you really are, then do what you need to do, in order to have what you want.

Margaret Young

Go confidently in the direction of your dreams. Live the life you have imagined.

Henry David Thoreau

It is hard to fail, but it is worse never to have tried to succeed.

Theodore Roosevelt

Our greatest glory consists not in never falling, but in rising every time we fall.

Oliver Goldsmith

Always be ready to speak your mind, and a base man will avoid you.

William Blake

We must have perseverance and above all confidence in ourselves.

Marie Curie

There is no failure except in no longer trying.

Elbert Hubbard

To be yourself in a world that is constantly trying to make you something else is the greatest accomplishment.

Ralph Waldo Emerson

The way to get started is to quit talking
and begin doing.

Walt Disney

*Do what you feel in your heart to be right
— for you'll be criticised anyway.*

Eleanor Roosevelt

Obstacles are those frightful things you see when you take your eyes off the goal.

Henry Ford

Small opportunities are often the beginning of great enterprises.

Demosthenes

Unless a man undertakes more than he possibly can do, he will never do all that he can.

Henry Drummond

Courage is resistance to fear, mastery of fear – not absence of fear.

Mark Twain

Life is either a daring adventure or nothing.

Helen Keller

A wise man will make more opportunities than he finds.

Francis Bacon

The question should be, is it worth trying to do, not can it be done.

Allard K. Lowenstein

Nothing is a waste of time if you use the experience wisely.

Auguste Rodin

When it is obvious that the goals cannot be reached, don't adjust the goals, adjust the action steps.

Confucius

I see my path, but I don't know where it leads. Not knowing where I'm going is what inspires me to travel it.

Rosalia de Castro

The first man gets the oyster, the second man gets the shell.

Andrew Carnegie

*One may walk over the
highest mountain one
step at a time.*

John Wanamaker

We are what we repeatedly do. Excellence, therefore, is not an act, but a habit.

Aristotle

There is a transcendent power in example.
We reform others unconsciously when
we walk uprightly.

Anne Sophie Swetchine

You see things and say 'Why?', but I dream things that never were; and I say 'Why not?'

George Bernard Shaw

In the middle of difficulty lies opportunity.

Albert Einstein

If you have built castles in the air, your work need not be lost; that is where they should be. Now put the foundations under them.

Henry David Thoreau

The power of imagination makes us infinite.

John Muir

Great things are not done by impulse, but by a series of small things brought together.

George Eliot

If you do not hope, you will not find what is beyond your hopes.

St Clement of Alexandra

*We are all inventors, each sailing out
on a voyage of discovery, guided each
by a private chart, of which there is no
duplicate. The world is all gates,
all opportunities.*

Ralph Waldo Emerson

What we truly and earnestly aspire to be,
that in some sense we are.

Anna Jameson

Go confidently in the direction of your dreams. Live the life you have imagined.

Henry David Thoreau

Optimism is the faith that leads to achievement. Nothing can be done without hope and confidence.

Helen Keller

A man's reach should exceed his grasp, or what's a heaven for?

Robert Browning

He is able who thinks
he is able.

Buddha

Without inspiration the best powers of the mind remain dormant, there is a fuel in us which needs to be ignited with sparks.

Johann Gottfried von Herder

Nothing is impossible to a willing heart.

John Heywood

The best way to make your dreams come true is to wake up.

Paul Valéry

*Every great dream begins with a dreamer.
Always remember, you have within you
the strength, the patience and the passion to
reach for the stars to change the world.*

Harriet Tubman

Your imagination is your preview of life's coming attractions.

Albert Einstein

What we plant in the soil of contemplation, we shall reap in the harvest of action.

Meister Eckhart

Sail away from the safe harbour. Catch the trade winds in your sails. Explore. Dream. Discover.

Mark Twain

You can break that big plan into small steps and take the first step right away.

Indira Gandhi

Destiny is no matter of chance. It is a matter of choice. It is not a thing to be waited for, it is a thing to be achieved.

William Jennings Bryan

*If we are facing in the right direction, all
we have to do is keep on walking.*

Buddha

To accomplish great things, we must not only act, but also dream; not only plan, but also believe.

Anatole France

*Dream lofty dreams, and as you dream,
so you shall become. Your vision is the
promise of what you shall one day be; your
ideal is the prophecy of what you
shall at last unveil.*

James Allen

Never give up, for that is just the place and time that the tide will turn.

Harriet Beecher Stowe

Have you enjoyed this book? If so, why not write a review
on your favourite website?

Thanks very much for buying this
Summersdale book.

www.summersdale.com